Zoo Animals

OTTERS
AT THE ZOO

By Seth Lynch

Gareth Stevens
PUBLISHING

Please visit our website, www.garethstevens.com. For a free color catalog of all our high-quality books, call toll free 1-800-542-2595 or fax 1-877-542-2596.

Library of Congress Cataloging-in-Publication Data

Names: Lynch, Seth, author.
Title: Otters at the zoo / Seth Lynch.
Description: New York : Gareth Stevens Publishing, [2020] | Series: Zoo animals | Includes index.
Identifiers: LCCN 2018039580| ISBN 9781538239384 (paperback) | ISBN 9781538239407 (library bound) | ISBN 9781538239391 (6 pack)
Subjects: LCSH: Otters–Juvenile literature. | Zoo animals–Juvenile literature.
Classification: LCC QL737.C25 L95 2020 | DDC 599.769–dc23
LC record available at https://lccn.loc.gov/2018039580

First Edition

Published in 2020 by
Gareth Stevens Publishing
111 East 14th Street, Suite 349
New York, NY 10003

Copyright © 2020 Gareth Stevens Publishing

Editor: Therese Shea
Designer: Katelyn E. Reynolds

Photo credits: Cover, p. 1 John And Penny/Shutterstock.com; p. 5 Anna Moskvina/Shutterstock.com; p. 7 (top left) Max Allen/Shutterstock.com; p. 7 (top right) Curioso/Shutterstock.com; p. 7 (bottom left) ostill/Shutterstock.com; p. 7 (bottom right) rbrown10/Shutterstock.com; p. 9 Maurice Volmeyer/Shutterstock.com; p. 11 Keneva Photography/Shutterstock.com; p. 13 Jennifer Krafsky/Shutterstock.com; pp. 15, 24 (tail) buteo/Shutterstock.com; pp. 17, 24 (webbed) guentermanaus/Shutterstock.com; p. 19 allixout/Shutterstock.com; p. 21 Kjersti Joergensen/Shutterstock.com; p. 23 © iStockphoto.com/shank_ali.

Printed in the United States of America

CPSIA compliance information: Batch #CS19GS: For further information contact Gareth Stevens, New York, New York at 1-800-542-2595.

Contents

I see otters at the zoo.
I learn a lot!

There are 13 kinds
of otters.

Most otters live near rivers.

The sea otter lives
in the ocean.

Otters swim well.

They have a flat tail.

They have webbed feet.

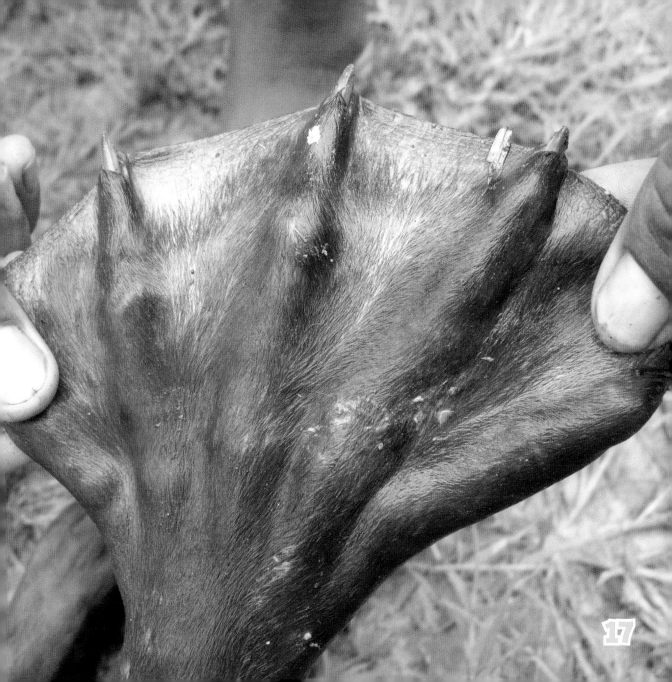

They have thick fur.
It keeps them warm.

Otters eat fish.
They eat other
water animals, too.

Otters love to play!
I like the otters
at the zoo!

Words to Know

tail

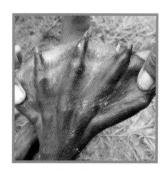
webbed

Index